PAT GRIGGS

with an introduction by
JIM ENDERSBY

JOSEPH HOOKER **BOTANICAL TRAILBLAZER**

Kew Publishing
Royal Botanic Gardens, Kew

HIGH TABLE LAND
THIBET.
Yangma
Kanglachema Pass
Kambachen
Yalloong
Nango
Junnoo
Kinchin-
Rungbo
Ruttoo
Rummam
Tongloo
10,079 ft.
Little Rungeet
Darjeeling
7165 ft.
Chumalari
23,929 ft.
Tumlong
Residence of Rajah.
J. D. H.
Notes
India
1848
Junnoo
&c

CONTENTS

INTRODUCTION BY JIM ENDERSBY

When Sir Joseph Hooker retired, in 1885, he was one of the most influential scientific men in the British Empire. As director of the Royal Botanic Gardens at Kew, he not only governed one of the country's foremost scientific institutions, advising government on many aspects of imperial policy, but also had unprecedented influence in appointing people to botanic gardens and other scientific posts around the world; a generation of British botanists owed their jobs more or less directly to Hooker's influence. His scientific service had brought him numerous honorary degrees, including ones from Oxford and Cambridge, and his research had been recognised by the Royal Society, which gave him their Royal (1854), Copley (1887) and Darwin (1892) Medals. He was also created Companion of the Bath, then Knight Commander of the Star of India, and Grand Commander of the Star of India, and eventually received the Order of Merit. He was, in many respects, a scientific emperor.

However, it's important to remember that Hooker wasn't always an emperor; he spent many years searching for a paid scientific position and had to rely on his father's influential friends to get many of the positions he did eventually secure. Most of Hooker's career was devoted to collecting and classifying; he named many new species and produced important floras for several parts of the world, but classification has never been a very glamorous or well-rewarded activity. Despite his importance there are aspects of Hooker's career and achievements that are fairly typical of many other now-forgotten Victorian men of science. Hooker is well known for his role at Kew and his long friendship with Darwin but in some ways the collecting and classifying aspects of his career that made him a typical Victorian man of science are just as important. By understanding Hooker, we understand some important things about how modern science came into existence.

When Joseph Hooker was born, on 30 June 1817 in Halesworth in Suffolk, there were no scientists; the word had not even been coined. By the time he died the modern scientist was an increasingly familiar sight, the proud possessor of a white coat and a university degree, working in a laboratory and funded by government or

WILLIAM HOOKER: A FATHER'S VIEW

'He has worked at plants with a degree of steadiness and ardour that has been most satisfying and it appears that his industry is likely to meet with its reward.'

Opposite Snow beds at 13,000 feet, in the Th'lonok Valley with rhododendrons in blossom. Kinchin-junga in the distance.

industry. Hooker didn't fit this picture at all, but his career, and those of men like him, would ensure that their successors would be scientists.

Both Hooker's father, Sir William Jackson Hooker (1785–1865), and his grandfather, Dawson Turner (1775–1858), were amateur naturalists who shared a passion for Britain's lower plants, such as mosses. However, in these early decades of the century, the word 'amateur' was a mark of pride. Far from being a hobbyist or dabbler, an amateur was one who pursued their study for the purest of reasons: love. By contrast, studying science with a view to earning a living from it was often considered rather distasteful, not least because any hint of financial self-interest would inevitably compromise the disinterestedness that ought to characterise the seeker after knowledge for its own sake.

This gentlemanly ideal of the scientific man was exemplified by Sir Joseph Banks who paid his own way and provided a substantial scientific staff in order to accompany Captain Cook on the *Endeavour* between 1768 and 1771. When Banks came home he was a famous explorer and became president of the Royal Society. A close friend of King George III he became *de facto* director of his majesty's scientific affairs, including the Royal Observatory, the Board of Longitude, the Board of Agriculture, and, from 1773, effective director of the Royal Gardens at Kew. Banks wielded considerable influence over scientific policy and appointments in Britain and around the world but he never received one penny from the King or anyone else for his work. His determination to work solely for the love of science and his nation was made possible by the fact that he had inherited the Revesby estate, which formed a significant percentage of Lincolnshire, and its rents brought him substantial personal wealth.

Rhododendrum barbatum, hand coloured lithograph by Fitch for *The Rhododendrons of Sikkim-Himalaya*, 1849–51.

COLLECTING RHODODENDRONS IN HIMALAYA

Hooker added 25 new species of rhododendrons to the 50 known at this time: 'Alas, one of my finest collections of Rhododendrons sent to Darjeeling got ruined by the coolies falling ill and being detained on the road, so I have to collect the troublesome things afresh. If your shins were as bruised as mine tearing through the interminable Rhododendron scrub of 10-13,000 feet you would be as sick of the sight of these glories as I am.'

William Hooker also inherited land from his father, but a much more modest estate than Revesby. His father-in-law, Dawson Turner, persuaded William to sell his land and invest the money in Turner's brewery and become its manager. This proved to be rather poor advice; Hooker didn't enjoy the brewing business and the depression that followed the end of the Napoleonic Wars in 1815 hit the brewery's profits badly. With a rapidly growing family, Hooker decided to turn his passion for botany into a paid position, as a university professor. He had no scientific degree (there were none available in Britain at the time), and – as Joseph would later comment

– William 'had never lectured, nor even attended a course of lectures'. But although Turner's business advice had been somewhat disastrous, he had at least managed to introduce Hooker to Banks and it was largely due to Banks's support that William Hooker was appointed as Regius Professor of Botany at the University of Glasgow in 1820.

Hooker's appointment at Glasgow was to be an important one for him, his son and, eventually, for British botany. He would use Glasgow as a base from which to build a global network of plant collectors and correspondents and also begin producing botanical publications of all kinds, from popular magazines for gardeners to technical monographs. His fame spread and, with the help of other influential connections, he eventually became the first director of Kew when it was brought under Government (as opposed to Royal) control in 1841. Nevertheless, in 1820 the move from brewery owner to botany professor was, in some important senses, a step down the social ladder. At Glasgow, Hooker worked for a meagre salary and had to stand at the door of his lecture theatre, collecting fees from students as they entered the room. Even worse, his students were medical students, at a time when doctors were often considered incompetent and greedy, more interested in keeping people ill, and thus paying fees, than in curing them. And as if that wasn't bad enough, many of Hooker's students were preparing to become apothecaries, the equivalent of today's pharmacists, who re-presented the lowest rung of the lowly medical profession because they were shopkeepers, engaging directly in trade with the public.

In the early decades of the century, there were almost no paying botanical positions in the UK that didn't involve teaching medical students. William Hooker supplemented his rather modest university income by publishing popular works for gardeners, but while they brought in some welcome money, the books and magazines tended to reinforce the lowly status of botany.

Joseph Hooker began his botanical education early, attending his father's lectures from the age of seven and

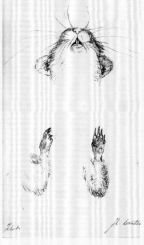

Tibet marmot. Hooker wrote: 'a species of marmot ("Kardiepieu" of the Tibetans) sometimes migrates in swarms (like the Lapland "Lemming") from Tibet as far as Tungu.'

going on field trips with students more than twice his age. He loved plants from childhood and never seriously considered a career that didn't revolve around botany. However, as he got older he became acutely aware that the practitioners of other sciences did not take botany very seriously. For the astronomers, physicists, chemists and geologists who were Britain's scientific elite, botany seemed a dull, undemanding business – little more than picking and pressing flowers – a pastime viewed at that time as more suitable for women and children than serious scientific men. So, when it came to choosing a career, Joseph Hooker had to improvise. He

Joseph Hooker's microscope.

Pages from Hooker's *Antarctic Journal* with watercolours of Mount Erebus and Mount Terror.

a large collection of exotic and unfamiliar specimens. As Hooker told his father, while waiting to set sail, 'No future Botanist will probably ever visit the countries whither I am going, and that is a great attraction' (3 February 1840).

Many Victorian men of science began their careers aboard ship; Darwin's travels on the HMS *Beagle* brought him to the attention of the leading scientific men of the day, and his collections were described and published by a team of eminent experts. His account of the voyage, *The Journal of Researches* (1839), the book we now know as *The Voyage of the Beagle*, also brought him a degree of public fame. While Hooker was waiting to set sail, a family friend gave him a copy of the proof-sheets of Darwin's book. He later recalled that he slept with the pages under his pillow so that he could carry on reading as soon as he woke and remembered that Darwin's book 'impressed me profoundly, I might say despairingly, with the variety of acquirements, mental and physical, required in a naturalist who should follow in Darwin's footsteps.'

Hooker would indeed follow in Darwin's footsteps, even visiting some of the countries the older naturalist described, but they travelled in very different styles. Darwin was not an official part of the *Beagle's* company; he was a gentleman companion to the ship's irascible and melancholic captain, Robert FitzRoy. Darwin's expenses were paid by his father and included a personal servant throughout the voyage. And because Darwin had no formal duties aboard ship he was able to spend almost two-thirds of the five-year voyage ashore, making lengthy journeys across South America collecting and studying its geology, while the *Beagle's* crew were hard at work on the ship's real business of surveying and making charts for the Admiralty. By contrast, Hooker

took a medical degree at Glasgow and used his father's influential contacts to secure a place aboard HMS *Erebus* which – accompanied by its sister ship HMS *Terror* – was about to set off on a four-year scientific voyage to the Antarctic. Despite being only a newly-qualified assistant surgeon Hooker asked the expedition's commander, Sir James Clark Ross, to appoint him as the expedition's botanist. Ross granted the rather meaningless title and assured Hooker that he would be given every opportunity to collect during the long Antarctic winters when the ships would need to retreat north to refit and resupply.

Travel was one of the few recognised routes to a scientific career in the early nineteenth century. The budding naturalist would often risk their life – Hooker was almost drowned on a couple of occasions – but if they survived they could hope to return, like Banks, with

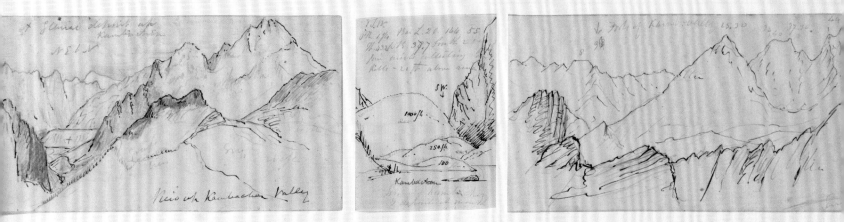

HOOKER'S FIRST EXPEDITION 1839–1843

'I am appointed from the Admiralty as Asst. Surgeon to the Erebus, and Capt. Ross considers me the Botanist to the Expedition and promises me every opportunity of collecting that he can grant.'

was a naval officer, responsible for the crew's health, expected to maintain discipline, to stand watch and help make the observations of the Earth's magnetic field that were the expedition's main purpose. His botanical collecting had to be done during the ship's relatively brief sojourns in places like New Zealand and Van Diemen's Land (Tasmania).

Hooker's early travels left him with a lifelong fascination with the geographical distribution of plants. Like earlier travellers, he saw that there were clear connections between the climate and latitude of a country and its characteristic plants. But what caused these connections? Was it climate or were there other reasons? Climate seemed unlikely to be the whole story because of various odd anomalies. For example, in some places, Hooker found closely related or identical species growing on islands separated by thousands of miles of apparently uncrossable ocean. Elsewhere he found completely unrelated species that nevertheless occupied identical places in the economy of nature (what we would now call the same ecological niches). These puzzling patterns could perhaps be explained by the geological history of the Earth, if, as the leading geologists of his day suggested, the land had risen and fallen dramatically in the past, joining and then disconnecting continents. The patterns of vegetation might be explained as the remnants of past migrations and extinctions. Hooker began to collect data on plant distribution in the hope of eventually understanding the scientific laws that explained the Earth's vegetation. However, he soon realised he would need much larger collections of plants from all over the world before he would be able to discern the patterns and test his hypotheses.

Watercolour and pencil sketch of
Rhododendrum barbatum by Joseph Hooker.

As the *Erebus* headed back towards England, after nearly four hard years in the southern oceans, Hooker wondered how he might get a position that would pay him to follow-up the purely scientific question of plant distribution. He was considering remaining in the Navy in the hope of receiving half-pay while he wrote-up his collections (Banks himself had persuaded the Admiralty to institute this policy) and wrote to his father to discuss this option. Joseph commented that 'as you know, I am not independent, and must not be too proud; if I cannot be a naturalist with a fortune, I must not be too vain to take honourable compensation for my trouble' (18 May 1843).

Hooker's letter makes it pretty clear that, given the choice, he would have preferred to be 'a naturalist with a fortune', like Banks. Instead of taking on the distinctly dubious status of 'professional' scientist, Hooker would have liked to be a wealthy amateur, like Darwin, free to pursue whatever topics interested him. But the lack of a sufficiently wealthy father ruled out this option and Hooker would spend the next decade searching for 'honourable compensation', and it's important to remember that finding a post that was 'honourable' – one that allowed him to take his place among the country's leading scientific gentlemen – was as important as finding sufficient compensation.

The Admiralty gave Hooker his half-pay and a grant towards the cost of publication, but it was scarcely enough to live on and would end once the publication was complete. So, he began looking for a more secure, better-paid position, which would also allow him to pursue his larger goals. His first attempt came in 1845, when he tried to become professor of botany at Edinburgh. His main rival was a local man, John Hutton Balfour, who made it clear that he was happy to teach the practical uses of

Sketches from Hooker's
Himalayan notebook.

botany, especially its medical ones. By contrast, Hooker made little secret of his disdain for teaching medicine: in a letter to his grandfather he referred to 'that lowest of all classes of students, the medical' (5 February 1845). If appointed professor, he hoped to turn the study of plants into a pure science, dealing with abstract, philosophical questions like distribution without regard to their practical applications. Hooker supplied an impressive collection of references all attesting to his ability, but his ambition cost him dearly; the Edinburgh Town Council, who controlled the appointment, chose the canny Balfour instead.

Hooker never made another attempt at getting a university post; he was touchy about his dignity and easily offended, but he also recognised that there was no demand for purely scientific botany in British universities at this time. His next job was at the Geological Survey (1846–47), which had provided the first government-funded scientific posts in Britain when it had been set up a decade earlier. Hooker took charge of fossil botany and published a few significant papers on fossil plants. But, from his perspective, the Survey was again hamstrung by its commitment to the practical uses of science; the very reason the Government funded it was that geology was vital to British industry, a national survey of the country's mineral wealth would help provide the coal and iron to keep industrialisation going. Hooker tried to persuade the Survey that it needed to create a comprehensive herbarium, a library of dried plants, which illustrated all Britain's living species. His justification was that this would provide an essential reference collection with which to identify fossil species, but of course it would also have allowed him to develop his real passion, studying plant distribution. The Survey refused to fund Hooker's grandiose scheme and he soon

Black Juniper
12,000 ft.

left to go travelling again.

Hooker would later describe his goal as being 'a general effort to lift Botany up in the scale of appreciated sciences' (letter to W. H. Harvey, December 1856). He realised early in his career that this would never happen if botany were only studied for its purely practical applications. Of course, he never lost sight of the uses of plants, including their medical ones. Throughout his travels, he would use the plants he found and his medical skills to treat the local people. And plants – from tea and opium to timber, spices and cotton – were the source of many valuable crops, upon which the British Empire's wealth rested. Understanding why particular plants grew in particular places was essential to knowing how valuable crops like rubber could be transplanted to British

Sketch and watercolour labelled 'black juniper' by Hooker from Himalayan notebook. Joseph described the use of juniper wood for temple incense and firewood: 'As the subject of fire-wood is of every-day interest to the traveller in these regions, I may here mention that the rhododendron woods afford poor fires; juniper burns the brightest, and with least smoke.'

colonies where they could be grown profitably. But the uses of plants were always a means to an end for Hooker; curing the locals was a way of gaining their trust so that they would help gather more specimens for Hooker's collection, and Kew's involvement in transplanting important crops helped justify the expense of its vast and ever-growing herbarium. However much Hooker enjoyed the prestige that came from getting *Cinchona* (the tree from which quinine was extracted) into India, one cannot help feeling that he would have studied plant distribution anyway, even if it had no practical uses at all.

After the disappointments of Edinburgh and the Geological Survey, Hooker made a second dangerous journey, to India (1847–51). Shortly before leaving, he had become engaged to Frances Henslow, the daughter of Darwin's old botany professor, John Stephens Henslow.

Illustration from the *Himalayan Journals*; Fitch's watercolour (*right*) drawn from Hooker's sketch and the final lithograph (*left*).

TRAVELS IN HIMALAYA

'My tent was made of a blanket thrown over the limb of a tree; to this others were attached, and the whole was supported on a frame like a house. One half was occupied by my bedstead, beneath which was stowed my box of clothes, while my books and writing materials were placed under the table. The barometer hung in the most out-of-the-way corner, and my other instruments all around.'

This meant that an income that would allow him to get married was becoming an urgent need. Frances must have been appalled when she heard the news that Hooker had been thrown in jail by the Rajah of Sikkim, the small princely state in the Himalaya in which he was travelling. There was great outrage in Britain and much sabre-rattling, which soon resulted in Hooker's release. However, the British newspaper reports of the 'outrage' did not mention that Hooker had brought his misfortunes on himself by deliberately ignoring the Rajah's orders that he must not cross the border into Tibet.

Despite the arrest, Hooker decided to spend two more years exploring the sub-continent, eventually returning to Britain in 1851 with a collection of about 7,000 species. William Hooker used his connections to secure a Government grant for Joseph to write up the results of his Indian travels. Thanks to the grant and the continuing support for the Antarctic publications, Joseph and Frances were finally able to marry in 1851, but it would be another four years before Hooker finally got a secure appointment at Kew, as assistant director to his father.

In addition to the first part of an uncompleted work on Indian botany (*Flora Indica*, 1855), Hooker had yet to complete his *Botany of the Antarctic Voyage*. The first volume, the *Flora Antarctica* (1844–7) had been completed before he left and he published its sequels – the floras of New Zealand (1851–3) and Tasmania (1853–9) – after his return. Working at Kew gave him access to his father's herbarium and library, but Hooker was always in need of more specimens and he relied on a scattered network of part-time, unpaid collectors to provide them.

During the *Erebus* voyage, Hooker had met some of his father's long-term correspondents, two of whom – William Colenso in New Zealand and Ronald Campbell Gunn in Tasmania – became life-long friends, vital sources of specimens, and provided introductions to other collectors in the colonies. Colenso was a missionary, who had been sent to New Zealand to print a Maori translation of the Bible, whereas Gunn was a convict supervisor (Van Diemen's Land was still a penal colony), but both men shared a love of plants. They were amateurs in the old fashioned sense; when Hooker complained of the problems he was having earning a living, Gunn replied that his 'account of the Rewards bestowed upon Science & learning in England is not encouraging', but added that 'it hardly required your letters to satisfy me that Natural History must be followed for its own sake alone by enthusiasts like ourselves' (26 September 1844). The enthusiasm of such collectors was vital to Hooker's work, especially since he had no way to pay them.

The crucial moment in Hooker's campaign to raise botany's status came in 1859, when his old friend Darwin finally published *On the Origin of Species*; here, at last, were natural history's scientific laws. Hooker had long known of Darwin's ideas and during the long years that Darwin kept his ideas to himself, he and Hooker had discussed them often, with Hooker offering both supporting evidence and well-informed criticism as the theory of evolution by natural selection took shape. Once

JOSEPH HOOKER TO CHARLES DARWIN

'From my earliest childhood I nourished and cherished the desire to make a creditable journey in a new country, and write such a respectable account of its natural features as should give me a niche amongst the scientific explorers of the globe I inhabit, and hand my name down as a useful contributor of original matter.'

ON

THE ORIGIN OF SPECIES

BY MEANS OF NATURAL SELECTION,

OR THE

PRESERVATION OF FAVOURED RACES IN THE STRUGGLE
FOR LIFE.

By CHARLES DARWIN, M.A.,

FELLOW OF THE ROYAL, GEOLOGICAL, LINNEAN, ETC., SOCIETIES;
AUTHOR OF 'JOURNAL OF RESEARCHES DURING H. M. S. BEAGLE'S VOYAGE
ROUND THE WORLD.'

LONDON:
JOHN MURRAY, ALBEMARLE STREET.
1859.

The right of Translation is reserved.

Darwin published, Hooker was the first man of science to publicly endorse the theory and he would become one of Darwin's most effective supporters. Nevertheless, Hooker worried about the impact of evolution on the practical business of classification. Colenso embraced Darwin's ideas eagerly, and Hooker worried that they might be taken as a justification for naming endless new species; after all if, as Darwin claimed, every variety of a plant was simply an 'incipient species', why not name them now, since they would be full species one day? To try and reign in those he regarded as over-eager species namers, Hooker stressed that Darwin's ideas would *not* change botany's practices, especially when it came to naming.

As Hooker's reputation grew, his authority and that of Kew grew as well. In 1865, William Hooker died and Joseph succeeded him as Kew's director. In 1868, he served as president of the British Association for the Advancement of Science and used his presidential address to give a ringing endorsement of Darwin's theories. In 1873, he became the first naturalist since Banks to preside over the Royal Society, one of the world's oldest and most prestigious scientific associations. His role as a 'botanical emperor' was finally secure, but it had not been achieved easily. It had taken many years of hard work to 'lift botany up in the scale of appreciated sciences'.

Part of Hooker's struggle was to be a gentleman first and a man of science second. Of course, the question of who should be considered a gentleman was a vexed one in Victorian Britain; many of the great novels of the period, such as Charles Dickens' *Great Expectations*, were explicitly preoccupied with the question of whether gentlemen were born or made. The men of science wanted to be rewarded without losing either the

27 St. James's Street. S.W.
April 24 1882
162

Sir Joseph,
    You are invited to officiate as one of the Pall Bearers at the Funeral of the late Mr Darwin which will take place at Westminster Abbey at 12 o'clock (noon) on Wednesday next the 26th inst.
    The Pall Bearers will assemble in the Chapter House in the Cloisters at 11.15 and we will arrange for some one to be there to meet you on arrival —
    We enclose a card of admission to the Chapter House, together with another card (which you will kindly also bring with you) indicating your position near the Remains
    We have the honor to be
        Your obedient Servants
        J. & W. Banting
            per J. W. Roche
        (Undertakers)
Sir Joseph Hooker. K. C. S. I.

Letter and 'card of admission' sent to Sir Joseph Hooker, inviting him to officiate as one of the pall bearers at the funeral of Charles Darwin in April 1882.

FUNERAL OF MR. DARWIN.

WESTMINSTER ABBEY,
Wednesday, April 26th, 1882.
AT 12 O'CLOCK PRECISELY.

Admit the Bearer at Eleven o'clock to the
CHAPTER HOUSE.
(Entrance by Dean's Yard.)
G. G. BRADLEY, D.D.
Dean.

N.B.—No Person will be admitted except in mourning.

Hooker at his desk in Sunningdale, 16 October 1906.

right Wedgwood plaque commemorating Sir Joseph Hooker in St Anne's Church, Kew Green. The plants were modelled by Matilda Smith and show some of his botanical interests.

the opportunities offered by the British Empire. The *Erebus* would never have sailed but for the needs of the Empire: the Government wanted accurate data to correct compass readings and it wanted the scientific prestige of demonstrating Britain's scientific leadership. Men like Colenso and Gunn would not have been in New Zealand or Australia if these hadn't been colonies, with convicts to supervise and natives to convert. And very few people would have cared about the floras of distant countries if so many of their plants hadn't proved so valuable to Britain's commerce. As these opportunities were developed and exploited, Kew became an empire in its own right, effectively governing a network of colonial botanic gardens around the world. However, it's worth noting that few of these gardens were set-up or funded by Kew; the Hookers used their skills and connections to befriend, persuade and cajole the gardens of Empire into joining their botanical enterprise, much as they persuaded individuals to collect for them. For most of its existence, Kew's empire was a rather fragile one, an improvised patchwork of friends and grateful recipients of metropolitan patronage, which had to keep demonstrating its usefulness to survive. When Joseph Hooker died, his widow was offered the option of burial in Westminster Abbey alongside Hooker's old friend, Darwin. However, she followed his wishes, and he was interred alongside his father in St Anne's Church on Kew Green, outside the gates of the Gardens they had created, and which had created them.

prestige and trust that had been placed in men like Sir Joseph Banks. Hooker never regarded his salary at Kew as making him into a public servant, but more as an honorarium paid by a grateful nation to someone who had served its needs disinterestedly. Science changed in the last decades of Hooker's life, becoming more specialised and requiring more training and equipment, such as purpose built laboratories. Hooker ensured that Kew got its first laboratory – the Jodrell – in 1877, but he never worked in it himself. As science changed and the word 'scientist' gradually began to be used in Britain, the old ideals of the gentleman were gradually transformed into the modern scientist's codes of conduct.

The other crucial part of Hooker's strategy to raise both his status and botany's was to take advantage of

JOSEPH DALTON HOOKER: NATURALIST, TRAVELLER AND MORE

In a letter to a friend, Joseph Hooker described himself as a 'naturalist and traveller'. But, as one of the most eminent botanists of the Victorian era, his activities were much more wide-ranging than this description would suggest, reflecting his many and various talents and interests.

Born in 1817, Joseph was the son of William Hooker, the first official director of the botanic gardens at Kew. From an early age, he was a keen botanist who published his first plant descriptions while still a student. Having qualified as a doctor, he began his travels in 1839 as an assistant surgeon on an arduous four-year voyage to the Antarctic. Before he had reached his mid-thirties, he was famous as a plant collector, not only for the thousands of Antarctic and Himalayan specimens he added to Kew's plant collections, but also for introductions of rhododendrons and other horticultural beauties. Throughout his travels, Joseph's skill as an artist was invaluable. His accurate botanical drawings recorded many of the plants he encountered, and the lively sketches in his journals and letters enchanted his family and friends.

When Joseph succeeded his father as director of the Royal Botanic Gardens, Kew, in 1865, he ensured that the Gardens retained their scientific focus and sustained their role as a centre for the transfer of crop plants around the British Empire. After his retirement from Kew in 1885, Sir Joseph, as he now was, continued to pursue his botanical interests. During a career spanning over 70 years, he identified more than 12,000 new plant species, often naming them in honour of friends and colleagues. His influential contributions to the understanding of plant relationships and plant distribution around the world were recognised by honours from scientific societies across the globe.

After his death in 1911, Joseph was buried next to his father in St Anne's churchyard at Kew. Inside the church, his memorial plaque illustrates five plants, representing a few of the diverse botanical passions of a man who was a 'naturalist and traveller' and much more.

opposite **Idealised portrait of J. D. Hooker during his Himalayan travels, c.1850.** Joseph Hooker described sitting for the original of this portrait, painted by William Tayler, the Postmaster General of Bengal in 1849: 'He is pleased to desire my sitting in the foreground surrounded by my Lepchas and the romantic-looking Ghorka guard, inspecting the contents of a vasculum full of plants, which I have collected during the supposed day's march.'

NATURALIST AND TRAVELLER

As a small boy, Joseph Hooker was captivated by Captain James Cook's descriptions of the distant lands he visited during his global voyages. At the age of 22, his dreams of travel were fulfilled when he joined the ship HMS *Erebus* as it set off on its four-year exploration of Antarctica. Ostensibly his role was that of 'Assistant Surgeon' but he preferred the title of 'Botanist to the Expedition'. He returned in 1843, with preserved plant specimens representing over 1,500 species, which he painstakingly studied over the next 20 years. Eventually he completed six illustrated volumes covering the plants of Antarctica, New Zealand and Tasmania.

In 1847, Joseph set off again, desirous of 'acquiring a knowledge of exotic botany'. His destination was India and the Himalayas of Nepal and Tibet. Over the next four years, he collected avidly, travelling alone or with fellow naturalists and British diplomats, through hazardous terrain and enduring considerable hardship. In Sikkim, he was thrown into prison and only released when the country's Rajah was threatened with 'severe retribution' from the British Army. Despite such setbacks, Hooker's Himalayan journeys were extremely fruitful. From Sikkim alone, he collected 25 new species of rhododendron, sending preserved specimens and seed back to Kew.

Subsequent journeys encompassed Morocco and the Atlas Mountains as well as Palestine and Syria. In 1877, during his final expedition, Joseph covered 8,000 miles across the USA in just 10 weeks. During a visit to the Californian groves of giant redwood, *Sequoiadendron giganteum*, he noted the threats these trees already faced from rising demand for timber.

Joseph's wide-ranging travels aroused his curiosity about plant distribution. For instance, why were some groups of plants found only in New Zealand, Australia and the southernmost parts of South America? His concept of a continent in the Southern Ocean where these species or their ancestors had arisen, was supported many decades later when evidence for the immense southern land-mass of Gondwana was discovered.

opposite **Kanchenjunga after a painting by William Tayler from B.H. Hodgson's bungalow.** Watercolour. Joseph Hooker enjoyed his stays with Brian Hodgson just outside Darjeeling. The views from the bungalow towards Kangchenjunga were awe-inspiring. Hooker wrote: 'The view from his windows is one quite unparalleled for the scenery it embraces, commanding confessedly the greatest known landscape of snowy mountains in the Himalaya and hence in the world.'

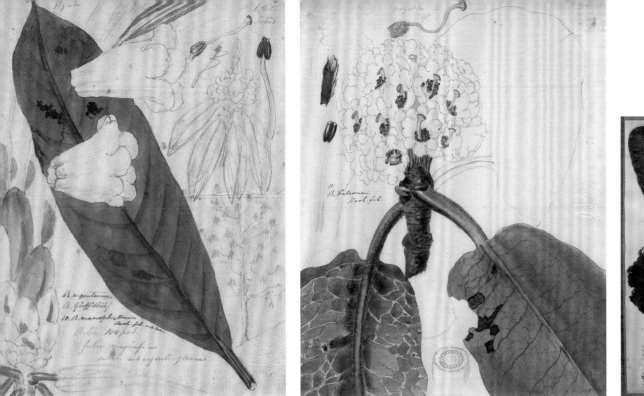

Joseph Hooker's field sketches formed the basis of W. H. Fitch's lithographs originally published in J. D. Hooker, *The Rhododendrons of Sikkim-Himalaya*, 1849.
Left **Rhododendron grande**, originally named *Rhododendron argenteum* by Joseph Hooker.
Centre **Rhododendron falconeri**. *Right* **Rhododendron setosum**.

As a talented artist, Joseph Hooker was able to capture the characteristics of many of the plants he found, either in pencil or watercolour. His sketches, combined with the dried pressed herbarium specimens he collected, were used by Walter Hood Fitch and other botanical artists, to produce illustrations for publication in books and scientific journals.

When he encountered *Rhododendron falconeri* during his ascent of Mount Tonglo, Hooker wrote: '*R. falconeri*, in point of foliage the most superb of all the Himalayan species, with trunks thirty feet high, and branches bearing at their ends only leaves eighteen inches long: these are deep green above and covered beneath with a rich brown down.' He found *Rhododendron setosum* growing at altitudes above 13,000 feet, and noted: 'after hot sunshine, [it] fills the atmosphere with its powerful aroma, too heavy by far to be agreeable; and it is indeed a sad aggravation to the discomforts of toiling in the rarified medium it inhabits. Covering, as it does, extensive moorland tracts and rocky slopes, the brilliant red purple of its flowers renders it a charming and most lovely object.'

'Looking south as evening drew on, another wonderful spectacle presented itself...I saw a sea of mist floating 3,000 feet beneath me, just below the upper level of the black pines; the magnificent spurs of the snowy range which I had crossed rising out of it in rugged grandeur as promontories and peninsulas, between which the misty ocean seemed to finger up like the fiords of Norway, or the salt-water lochs of the west of Scotland...'

Sketches from Hooker's Himalayan notebooks, Sheet 44. Joseph Hooker sketched the view from the Choonjerma Pass (*below*) in Nepal and it was later reproduced in watercolour by Walter Hood Fitch (*right*) for the published *Himalayan Journals*. The peak marked 'very high snows NNW' is believed to be Everest (or Mount Chomolungma as it is known locally), and this drawing, which dates from 1848, may be the earliest western illustration of the world's highest mountain.

Sea of mist from 16000 ft elevⁿ
from Choonjerma Pass.

W. Fitch.

top of Choonjerma Pass.
looking West over Nepal snows.

Sketches from Hooker's Himalayan notebooks, Sheet 76. When Joseph Hooker reached the Donkia Pass (*bottom*, sketch by Hooker, watercolour by Walter Hood Fitch *above*), and saw the landscape around the Cholamoo lakes, he wrote 'though my solitary situation rendered it doubly impressive to me, I doubt whether the world contains any scene with more sublime associations than this calm sheet of water, 17,000 feet above the sea, with the shadows of mountains 22,000 to 24,000 feet high, sleeping on its bosom.'

***Magnolia cathcartii* by Indian artist employed by J. F. Cathcart.** Cathcart was a retired British judge from the Bengal Civil Service, who Joseph Hooker encountered in Darjeeling. He employed local plant collectors to scour the mountains for plants for his team of Indian artists to illustrate. Joseph gave the artists some training in drawing floral dissections. Walter Hood Fitch later lithographed the illustrations which were published in *Illustrations of Himalayan Plants* with descriptions by Joseph himself.

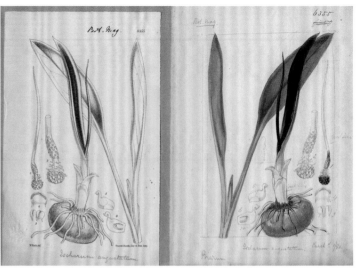

left **Apteranthes europaea var. europaea by W. H. Fitch, 1874.** Joseph Hooker encountered this plant on a rocky island near the port of Mogador in southern Morocco. In his *Journal of A Tour in Marocco and the Great Atlas*, he recorded the effect of a plague of locusts which had stripped the island of plants so that 'scarcely a green leaf remained.' He observed that 'In such a spot we expected to find the coast vegetation fully developed, but we counted without the locusts.'

above **Biarum angustatum by W. H. Fitch, 1878.** This arum was collected during a tour of Lebanon, Syria and Palestine in the autumn of 1860. Hooker collected the plant as a dormant tuber and was unable to identify it until it flowered at Kew; 'I cannot tell exactly where, for the tubers were collected in Sept., without any flowers, and put into a bag with many other roots that I dug up as I journeyed along, and to whose generic name even I then had no clue.'

below **Sempervivum atlanticum by W. H. Fitch, 1873.** This houseleek was found in the valley of Ait Mesan in the High Atlas, where Joseph Hooker and his companions collected 375 species in just six days. Joseph was particularly keen to 'become acquainted with' the vegetation of the High Atlas, and 'to ascertain whether this supplied connecting links between that of the Mediterranean region and the peculiar flora of the Canary Islands.'

right **Salvia taraxacifolia by W. H. Fitch, 1872.** This ornamental sage was found growing among rock along riverbeds near Tasseremout in Morocco. Joseph Hooker wrote: 'It was collected by Messrs Ball, Maw and myself in 1871, growing on rocks and shingle in beds of rivers along the base of the Greater Atlas, at elevations of 2,000 to 3,000 feet, sometimes forming broad patches, and presenting a very beautiful appearance.'

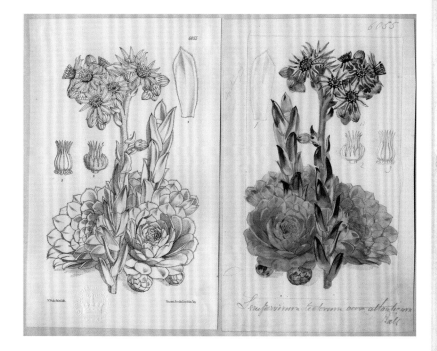

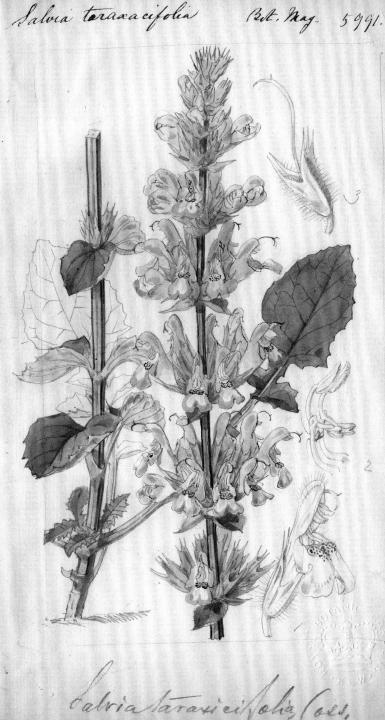

M Smith del.

M.S.del, J.N.Fitch lith.

Vincent Brooks,Day & Son Lt.

L. Reeve & C.º London.

Epilobium obcordatum, A. Gray.

Epilobium obcordatum, A. Gray.

opposite **Epilobium obcordatum by Matilda Smith, 1899.** This American species had been named and described by Asa Gray, who was one of Joseph Hooker's oldest friends and correspondents. Joseph described it as 'decidedly the most attractive species of the genus in cultivation, if not in nature; and as a rock garden plant it has few rivals.' He collected the plant in fruit in September 1877 from 'Rocky places on Mt Stanford, above Truckee, where the railroad crosses the Sierra Nevada.'

TRAVELS IN AMERICA

'I have indeed had a splendid journey; and thanks to A. Gray a most profitable one—nothing could or can ever reach his unwearied exertions to make me master of all I saw throughout the breadth and not a little of the length of the U. States. The Geographical Distribution of the Flora is wonderfully interesting, and its very outlines are not yet drawn…. I have brought home upwards of 1,000 species of dried specimens for comparison of the Rocky and Sierra Nevada and Coast Range Floras, an investigation of which should give the key to the American Flora migrations.'

Damnamenia vernicosa by W. H. Fitch, 1844 Joseph Hooker described this species as 'a very handsome plant' when he encountered it on the sub-Antarctic islands during his travels on HMS *Erebus*. It was one of the plants chosen to represent his botanical interests on his memorial plaque in St Anne's Church on Kew Green.

Cyathea medullaris, lithograph from W. J. Hooker's *Garden Ferns* by W. H. Fitch, 1862. During his Antarctic voyage on the HMS *Erebus*, Joseph Hooker visited New Zealand in 1841. The ship anchored in the Bay of Islands at the tip of North Island. In his *Handbook of New Zealand Plants*, published between 1864 and 1866, he described over 120 species of ferns, including this black tree fern.

Indian notebook, Junnoo, 1848

Sketch by Joseph Hooker from Himalayan
notebook, Tungu Chomiomo,1849

Aptenodytes demersa

Sketch by Joseph Hooker from
Antarctic Journal, f.91v 18 May
1839–28 Mar 1843

Sea bears the Otaria ursina is the only animal that ever is seen on shore, the young dogs are constantly coming up on the beach & barking in the summer very few females were seen. Sperma cati whales are very common often come into the bay when after plundering & playing about for some time they run into deep waters throw their tails up in the air & disappear. True seals were any to the northern whilst I have seen one very abundant here but during our stay we have seen none, nor any sea elephants.

Birds there are a good many species all but one sea birds during our stay here. Specimens were collected most of them were very common 1. Chionis vaginalis? the sheath bill I doubt if this is the same as the true Holland bird, the forehead is not bare, the sheath is not bare on the bill nor is the bill so broad & large as that of the figure in Rees Cyclopedia. It is all over of a pure white, the young bird with pink tips to the wings, eyes black with a red caruncula, eyelid beak black, legs flesh red. The head is much laterally compressed & the forehead high. On the ...

...the inner bone of the wing there is a small wart, the articulation of the spine. It is referred to the Gralla by Cuvier, it runs with great agility among the large loose rocks along the shore aiding itself down the declivities by the wings when they want pinions against the rock. It is very tame, seldom flies, when it does it invariably utters a low sharp croak as it rises on the wing, when hard pursued it takes to the water but this very seldom & swims slowly. They are so tame that you may approach within a yard of them when they move quietly out of the way, curiosity is a predominant trait in their feature with them if you sit down they will gather round & examine you very minutely, singing & whistling seems to delight them much when they will come & sit perch on your foot nicking their heads on one side in the most interesting manner. From their tameness they formed a constant prey to our sailors & sportsmen with a gun they are hard to kill flying away with a charge of shot quite uncommonly. Their food is any thing they can get especially dead carrion. As food they are tolerable eating rather tough though they have a rank flavor & smell when newly killed & require soaking before looking when they eat well in pies & Mulligatawny stews. When kept on board if given the scraps of the deck they get very tame eating & drinking literally every thing when put in cages they spend all their strength & energies in ineffectual attempts to escape & if 2 or more are together they fight like Game cocks till one survives here they soon get very dirty on board. I suspect they feed among the rats.

2. Aptenodytes demersa the common Jack Ass penguin is one of the most amusing birds there. They come up in flocks out of the sea & waddle along the shore doing nothing but standing upright & looking at one another. To catch them you must run between them...

Sketch by Joseph Hooker,
Moroccan notebook,1871

Clinometer

Field barometer

MEASURING INSTRUMENTS

'I have not lost or broken a
single instrument during my
journey, though I have had
8 thermometers in daily use,
2 barometers, 2 chronometers,
3 compasses, a sextant, and
Artificial Horizon. I consider
this quite a feat always
remembering the roads to be
of the worst, and that 50 men
were bustling about me all
day long.'

National Antarctic Expedition,

University Building,

Burlington Gardens, W.

TELEGRAPHIC ADDRESS:
"ANTARCTIC, LONDON."

May 21st

Dear Sir Joseph Hooker

It was your suggestion that and the great weight of your practical Experience alone that caused me to really consider a balloon equipment as a practical possibility. I took the liberty of using your name in this connection when writing to the war office ... not like to do so when writing publicly ... your permission, which ... not time to get.

... you very much for your support — I hope ... shall manage to secure ... wish

Kind regards to

Hooker

believe me

Yours sincerely

R.V. Scott

Letter from Captain Robert Scott (Scott of the Antarctic), 21 May 1901. This reads: 'It was your suggestion and the great weight of your practical experience alone that caused me to really consider a balloon equipment as a practical possibility. I took the liberty of using your name in this connection when writing to the war office but did not like to do so when writing publicly without your permission, which I had not time to get. Thank you very much for your generous support. I hope we shall manage to realise our wish. With kind regards to Lady Hooker.'

Naturalist and Traveller 33

JOSEPH HOOKER'S LEGACY: THE UK OVERSEAS TERRITORIES

Throughout his career, one of Joseph Hooker's particular interests, sparked by his journey to the Antarctic on HMS *Erebus* (1839–43), was the origin of island plants. Among the islands where he was able to collect plant specimens were St Helena and Ascension, isolated in the middle of the southern Atlantic, and the Falkland Islands, off the southernmost tip of South America. These islands are now UK Overseas Territories (UKOTs), which remain part of the United Kingdom.

When Joseph visited them, both St Helena and Ascension had already been colonised for several centuries, providing safe anchorage for ships on long trans-Atlantic voyages. Joseph later described St Helena in a lecture on island floras: 'When discovered, about 360 years ago, it was entirely covered with forests .... Now all is changed, fully 5/6ths of the island are utterly barren... The indigenous flora is almost confined to a few patches towards the summit of Diana's Peak, the central ridge, 2,700 feet above the sea.' Goats, introduced to the island by sailors, caused most deforestation, browsing voraciously on the vegetation and killing off seedlings. Exotic plants, imported by settlers as crops

While the HMS *Erebus* spent a long Antarctic winter in safe harbour in the Falkland Islands, Joseph had plenty of opportunity to investigate the plants of the islands. He reported to his father about the grazing potential of tussac grass, *Poa flabellata*, which formed much of the coastal grassland on the islands.

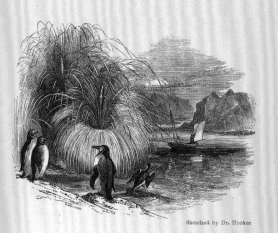

Sketched by Dr. Hooker.

Tussac Grass of Falkland Islands. Page 270.

CHAPTER VIII.

Magnificent Range of Bergs. — Colour of the Sea. — North-easterly Gale. — Recross the Antarctic Circle. — Collision with the Terror. — Loss of Bowsprit — the Stern-board. — The Escape. — Unusual Phenomenon. — Repair Damages. Focus of Greater Intensity. — Circle of Mean Temperature of the Ocean. — Meteorological Abstract for March. — Current off Cape Horn. — Beauchêne Island. — Anchor in Port Louis, East Falkland Island.

II.

and ornamentals or held in transit through the botanic garden, escaped from cultivation and overwhelmed the island's unique native plants.

Despite observing the detrimental effect of introduced plants on St Helena, Joseph advised the British Admiralty to establish various trees, grasses and crop plants to Ascension to increase rainfall and help soil formation on the island, which he described as 'a scorched mass of volcanic matter'. The Admiralty hoped to improve conditions for the island's army garrison, located there to protect the island from French forces attempting to rescue Napoleon Bonaparte from St Helena. Joseph recorded his fears about the project, stating 'the consequences to the native vegetation of the Peak will, I fear, be fatal, and especially to the rich carpet of ferns that clothed the top of the mountain when I visited it.'

Over 150 years later, Kew's UK Overseas Territories programme provides practical and technical support for partner organisations on St Helena, Ascension and the Falkland Islands who are working to conserve and restore the islands' natural vegetation. Projects in all three Territories have identified and mapped native species and assessed threats from invasive exotic plants, pests and other factors.

Plant specimens that Joseph collected in these three UKOTs in the 1840s have been digitised and incorporated into an online herbarium for use by botanists and conservationists within the Territories. They provide the concrete proof of the presence of particular species at a specific site on a specific date, needed for conservation assessments. So Joseph Hooker's legacy of specimen collections lives on as an invaluable resource which will inform efforts to conserve the very species he discovered and documented.

Kew's horticulturists have helped to develop propagation techniques for St Helena's threatened unique plants, including *Mellissia begonifolia*. Joseph Hooker named this species in 1867 in honour of James Melliss, a government official who had botanised on the island. He believed it was 'very rare and probably now already extinct in the wild'. In 2008, conservationists on St Helena discovered a few plants growing on a rocky slope. Some of the seeds collected from these plants have been stored in the Millennium Seed Bank whilst others have been germinated in Kew's nursery glasshouses. About 13,000 seeds from the plants grown at Kew have been sent back to St Helena.

Across its 800 islets and islands, the Falklands have 13 species of unique plants, all adapted to survive the harsh winds and cold winters. Teams of Kew staff have assisted Falklands Conservation in mapping and monitoring the locations of these plants to define Important Plant Areas on the islands as a focus for future conservation activities, such as invasive plant clearance and grazing management. Seeds from several Falklands species have been germinated to produce plants for display in Kew's Rock Garden.

On Ascension, conservationists rediscovered the Ascension Island parsley fern, *Anogramma ascensionis*, originally described by Joseph in 1843. After tending the small population of ferns on their fragile cliff face, the team collected fronds with spores which were rushed to Kew's Conservation Biotechnology Section, who successfully germinated the spores to produce new plants.

Tab. 1.

Hodgsonia heteroclita. Hk.f. ♂

Hodgsonia heteroclita. Hk.f. ♀

FAMILY MAN, FRIEND AND COLLEAGUE

By dedicating his life to collecting, studying and promoting the importance of plants, Joseph Hooker was following a great family tradition. Shortly after his birth in 1817, his father, William, became professor of botany at Glasgow University and subsequently, from 1841, the first director of the botanic gardens at Kew. Joseph's maternal grandfather was a moss enthusiast, who was acquainted with many important botanists, including Sir Joseph Banks who had travelled with Captain Cook. His first wife, Frances, was the daughter of John Stevens Henslow, the Cambridge professor of botany who had taught Charles Darwin, the famous naturalist. Joseph was a devoted family man; he had nine children during his two marriages.

Charles Darwin became one of Joseph's closest friends. They met in 1839, just before Joseph set out for Antarctica, and remained in regular contact for over 40 years, on both scientific and family matters. In their letters, they discussed Darwin's theories about the adaptability of species and mechanisms of evolution. Joseph encouraged Darwin to present his theories about species evolution at the Linnean Society, one of Britain's most prestigious scientific organisations. Later, in 1859, he was one of Darwin's staunchest supporters when controversy erupted with the publication of the book, *On the Origin of Species*.

Another long-standing friend was the American botanist, Asa Gray, from the Harvard Herbarium, who Joseph had met in 1839. The two men had a common interest in plant distribution, which they explored in detail during Joseph's tour of the USA in 1877. For over twenty years, Joseph worked closely with the botanist George Bentham to produce *Genera Plantarum*, a classification of all known plant genera, which was, until recently, used to organise plant collections in many of the world's herbaria and botanic gardens.

Joseph's relationships with his colleagues were not always cordial. He quarrelled with Walter Hood Fitch, the talented botanical artist and lithographer who, over 40 years, had produced illustrations for many of the publications Joseph and his father had written. Although Fitch ceased producing illustrations for *Curtis' Botanical Magazine*, which Joseph edited, their relationship became more amicable after Joseph managed to arrange a pension for the artist.

Hodgsonia macrocarpa, left **male, and** *right* **female flower by J. D. Hooker.** Joseph wrote: 'This magnificent plant is one of the most curious and beautiful of the whole natural family to which it belongs, and was therefore selected by Dr Thomson and myself to bear the name of B. H. Hodgson, Esq., F.L.S., of Dorjiling, in the Sikkim-Himalaya, a gentleman whose scientific services in the Himalaya of Nipal and Sikkim justly merit this honour, and in whose hospitable residence my examination of this splendid plant was conducted.' Joseph stayed with Brian Hodgson just outside Darjeeling and described him as 'a great naturalist who is ill and nervous to such a degree that he fancies the Darjeeling doctors want to kill him, and he will have no other medical attendant than myself.'

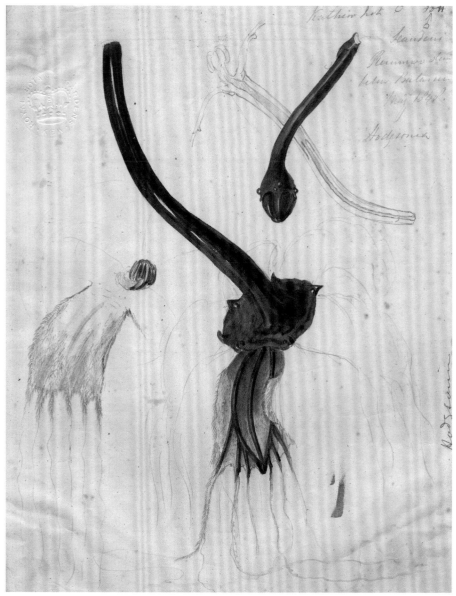

Hodgsonia macrocarpa, sketches by J. D. Hooker *left*, **and Indian artist employed by J. F. Cathcart**. Joseph Hooker described *Hodgsonia macrocarpa* in his Himalayan Journal: 'But the most magnificent plant of these jungles is *Hodgsonia*, (a genus I have dedicated to my friend, Mr Hodgson), a gigantic climber allied to the gourd, bearing immense yellowish-white pendulous blossoms, whose petals have a frings of buff-coloured curling threads, several inches long.'

left **Fruits of *Hodgsonia macrocarpa*, sketches by J. D. Hooker.** Alongside his sketches and dried specimens, Joseph Hooker took detailed notes about the plants he found, including descriptions of their local uses: 'The great melon-like fruit, called 'Kathior-pot' by the Lepchas, ripens in autumn and winter. Its coarse, hard, green pulp exudes a gummy fluid in great abundance, but is austere and uneatable.'

Fruits and seeds of *Hodgsonia macrocarpa*, W. H. Fitch lithograph.

Sir Joseph and Lady Hooker in their home, The Camp, Sunningdale, December 1904. After the death of his first wife Frances in 1874, Joseph Hooker married Hyacinth Jardine, the widow of another distinguished naturalist, in 1876. Around their home at The Camp, Hooker planted specimens of many of the rhododendrons he had collected in Sikkim.

CHARLES ROBERT DARWIN
LL.D., F.R.S., F.L.S.
Born 1809.   Died 1882.

Charles Darwin, c.1870s. Charles Darwin and Joseph Hooker met and corresponded regularly for over 40 years. One of Darwin's legacies to his friend was funding for the publication of *Index Kewensis,* a comprehensive listing of all the names of the world's plant species. Kew continues to update this essential botanical resource so that botanists around the world have access to all newly published plant names.

The words on the frame read 'I like this photograph very much better than any other which has been taken of me.' signed 'Ch. Darwin'

opposite **Encampment in the Rockies, La Veta Pass, Colorado, at 9,000 feet, 25 July 1877.** Shortly after receiving his knighthood in 1877, Sir Joseph (seated left) set off for an extended visit to the United States, to meet up with his friend Professor Asa Gray (seated on ground) for a plant collecting trip to Colorado, Utah and California. The two men were keen to investigate the differences between the plants found in the eastern and western states of the USA. Joseph wrote of his friend 'Gray is a man of extraordinary energy and though 5 or 6 years my senior is the younger of the two!'

Seated from left to right are Sir Joseph Hooker, Professor Asa Gray, Mrs Richard Strachey, Mrs Asa Gray, Dr Robert Henry Lambourne, Major-General Richard Strachey and Dr F. V. Hayden.

Portrait of Sir Joseph Dalton Hooker by Theodore Blake Wirgman, 1886. By this time Hooker had officially retired as Director of the Royal Botanic Gardens, Kew. In a letter to Asa Gray after his retirement, he observed: 'I am deep in India laurels (they are perfectly dreadful). I have just sent Bentham's Flora to press. I am on the councils of the Royal and Geographical, and I have to find time for bed and meals – I forgot that I have the Bot. Mag. ever before me too.'

CURTIS'S
BOTANICAL MAGAZINE,
COMPRISING THE
Plants of the Royal Gardens of Kew
AND
OF OTHER BOTANICAL ESTABLISHMENTS IN GREAT BRITAIN,
WITH SUITABLE DESCRIPTIONS.

BY
JOSEPH DALTON HOOKER, M.D., F.R.S. L.S. & G.S.,
K.C.S.I., C.B., LL.D. OXFORD, CORRESPONDENT OF THE INSTITUTE OF FRANCE

VOL. XXII.
OF THE THIRD SERIES;
(Or Vol. XCII. of the Whole Work.)

LONDON:
L. REEVE & CO., 5, HENRIETTA STREET, COVENT GARDEN.
1866.

BOTANICAL MAGAZINE

Established in 1787, *Curtis's Botanical Magazine* is the world's oldest colour-illustrated periodical. Throughout its history it has featured plants of horticultural interest, many of them recently introduced to cultivation. Joseph Hooker took over as editor of the Magazine in 1865 on the death of his father and continued until 1904. It is still published by Kew.

***Rosa pisocarpa* by Matilda Smith, 1886.** Joseph Hooker and Asa Gray collected *Rosa pisocarpa* in California during their whistle-stop tour of the south-western states of the USA. Asa Gray wrote to a friend: 'But never were such busy people as Hooker and I the whole time. In fact, I was bound to make Hooker see just as much as possible within our limited time, and it seemed on the whole best for us to see very much in glimpses and snatches rather than far less more leisurely and thoroughly.'

Sir William Thiselton-Dyer and Lady Harriet Thiselton-Dyer, Kew, late 19th century. Joseph Hooker's eldest daughter, Harriet *far left*, married William Thiselton-Dyer, who had been her father's assistant and then became his successor as Director of the Royal Botanic Gardens, Kew. Thiselton-Dyer was a plant physiologist by training. He took responsibility for the establishment of the Jodrell Laboratory at Kew, which provided facilities for studies of plant structures and chemicals.

Matilda Smith and Walter Hood Fitch. Walter Hood Fitch was the principal artist for *Curtis's Botanical Magazine*, under the editorship of both William and Joseph Hooker, from 1860 until 1878, contributing over 2,900 illustrations. He was succeeded by Matilda Smith, many of whose illustrations were lithographed by Fitch's nephew, John Nugent Fitch.

Etlingera elatior **by William Jackson Hooker, 1832.**
Joseph Hooker's father, William, was himself a
talented botanical artist. He drew the flowering
head of this spectacular member of the ginger family
(Zingiberaceae) for *Curtis's Botanical Magazine*
to accompany the detailed description of the plant
which he had written.

**Portrait of Sir William Jackson Hooker by Spiridone
Gambardella, 1909.** Joseph Hooker's father, William,
became the first official director of the botanic gardens
at Kew in 1841. Among his notable achievements
as director were the construction of the Palm and
Temperate Houses, and the establishment of the
world's first museum of economic botany.

Fallugia paradoxa pencil and watercolour by Anne Barnard, 1882, with John Nugent Fitch lithograph.
Anne Barnard was one of several of Joseph Hooker's family connections who produced illustrations for *Curtis's Botanical Magazine*. She was the youngest sister of Joseph's first wife, Frances. Joseph had collected this plant in Southern Colorado on his journey around the western states of the USA, saying 'the copious large white blossoms on the slender branches, moving with the slightest breath of wind, gave the bushes a very beautiful appearance.'

right **Cornus capitata, originally named *Dendrobenthamia capitata*, by W. H. Fitch, 1852.**
This Nepalese plant was originally named after George Bentham, one of the most important botanists of the Victorian era, who worked extensively with Joseph Hooker on a classification of the flowering plants and ferns which was published as *Genera Plantarum*. Bentham donated his personal herbarium of preserved plant specimens to Kew, representing over 50,000 species.

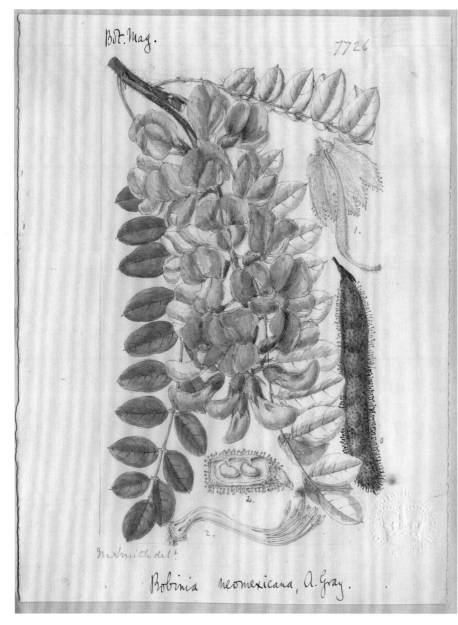

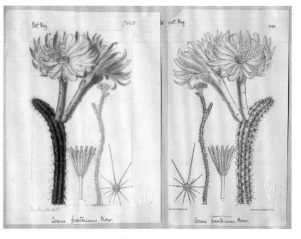

Praecereus euchlorus by Matilda Smith, 1899. This cactus was drawn by Matilda Smith who became the principal artist for *Curtis's Botanical Magazine* after Walter Hood Fitch withdrew his services. She was Joseph Hooker's second cousin and had been trained by him in botanical drawing.

Robinia neomexicana by Matilda Smith, 1900. Joseph Hooker found *Robinia neo-mexicana* while he was travelling with Asa Gray, who was professor of natural history at Harvard University. He noted: 'I collected *R. neo-mexicana* in fruit, when visiting the Rocky Mountains, in company with Dr Gray, near the town of La Veta in Colorado. The tree, from which the specimen figured was taken, has been in cultivation in the Kew Arboretum for the last twelve years, flowering in June. It was received from the Botanic Gardens of Harvard, USA in 1887.'

***Musa bakeri* by Matilda Smith, 1898.** Joseph Hooker named this plant after J. G. Baker who was Keeper of Kew's Herbarium. Baker, who wrote most of the descriptions of monocotyledonous plants for *Curtis's Botanical Magazine*, described how this plant 'flowered for the first time in the palm-stove of the Royal Gardens, Kew in 1895', just five years after it had been received from the Jardin des Plantes at Paris.

***Northolirion macrophyllum* by Harriet Thiselton-Dyer, 1878.** Harriet Thiselton-Dyer, Joseph Hooker's eldest daughter, was a skilled botanical artist. In 1905, Sir William Thiselton-Dyer, then Kew's Director, dedicated the annual volume of *Curtis's Botanical Magazine* to 'my wife Harriet, Lady Thiselton-Dyer, whose grandfather and father have successively edited the 'Botanical Magazine for three quarters of a century and whose skilful pencil has contributed to its many illustrations.'

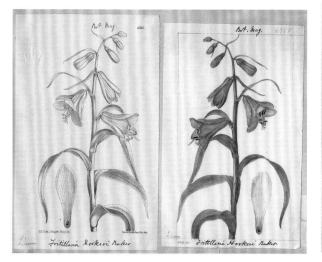

Letter from Joseph Hooker to Professor Asa Gray, Harvard University, 24 March 1854. This was written before Hooker even became assistant director of Kew; he was somewhat disgruntled by the lack of funding or recognition for his botanical research on behalf of Kew and had been searching for botanical posts elsewhere.

Letter from Joseph, in Darjeeling, to his sister Elizabeth, April 1849. The sketch shows Hooker's dog 'Kinchin', a cross between a 'Thibet mastiff and Lepcha hunting dog', writing with pen on paper. The letter recounts how he was acquired as young puppy, how clever he is and the mischief he gets up to stealing food from the camp kitchen.

Medal awarded 'To Sir Joseph Dalton Hooker in recognition of his services to science from the Linnean Society of London 1898'.

left Letter from Charles Darwin requesting seeds, 17 October 1879.

right Letter to Charles Darwin regarding Darwin's 'species concept', 6 & 7 April 1850.

MARRIAGE TO FRANCES HENSLOW

'I believe Miss Henslow to be an amiable and well-educated person of most respectable, though not high connections, and from all that I have seen of her, well suited to Joseph's habits and pursuits. He himself seems well pleased with his choice.'

William Hooker

Marriage licence to Frances Henslow, 8 July 1851.

CHARLES EVANS, Master of Arts, Vicar General in Spirituals of the Right Reverend Father in God SAMUEL, by Divine Permission, LORD BISHOP of Norwich, and Official Principal of the Episcopal Consistorial Court of Norwich lawfully constituted: To our beloved in Christ, *Joseph Dalton Hooker* of the Parish of *Mollake* in the County of *Surrey* a *Bachelor* of the age of *twenty one years and upwards* and *Frances Harriet Henslow* of the Parish of *Hitcham* in the County of *Suffolk within our Jurisdiction* a *Spinster* of the age of *twenty one years and upwards* Health and Grace. Whereas it is alledged, that Ye have resolved to proceed to the Solemnization of true and lawful Matrimony

DIRECTOR OF KEW AND SCIENTIFIC FIGUREHEAD

Although Joseph Hooker had added greatly to Kew's living plant collections, notably in the Rhododendron Dell, and its herbarium, with plants from Antarctica and the Himalaya, it was not until 1855 that his father's efforts on his behalf paid off and he was appointed assistant director at Kew. Just 10 years later, when Sir William Hooker died, Joseph took over as director of the Royal Botanic Gardens, Kew. Under his aegis, the trees in the Arboretum and the plants in the Herbaceous Ground, now the Order Beds, were laid out according to the Bentham-Hooker classification, which he had developed in collaboration with George Bentham. Notable additions to the Gardens were the Jodrell Laboratory and the North Gallery, the latter containing over 800 paintings donated by the redoubtable Victorian artist and traveller, Marianne North.

All did not go smoothly however; a dispute with the government minister responsible for Kew threatened the Gardens' scientific activities. The minister, Acton Smee Ayrton, undermined Joseph's authority as director and supported a proposal to remove Kew's herbarium collection of preserved plants. He saw Kew's role as primarily for 'the instructive pleasure of the public'. The dispute was resolved in 1873, when over 50 eminent scientists supported a recommendation for separate herbaria at the Natural History Museum and at Kew.

Kew's colonial activities continued under Joseph's auspices. The Gardens advised on crop plants suitable for various colonies and helped to acquire seeds or cuttings. Joseph and his father had initiated the successful transfer of quinine trees from South America to India. Subsequently rubber trees were introduced from Brazil to India, and then disease-resistant coffee plants from West Africa to Sri Lanka.

Joseph's contributions to the nation's botanical science were rewarded when the Queen awarded him the Companion of the Bath (CB) in 1869, and later the title of Knight Commander of the Order of the Star of India, an honour he much prized. His scientific achievements were recognised by his election to the Presidency of the Royal Society (1873–8), and medals from botanical and horticultural societies around the world.

opposite **The Kew Gardens Question, cartoon, c.1876.** Throughout his directorship, Joseph Hooker faced public demands for more access to the Gardens, which were only open to ordinary visitors in the afternoons. The mornings were reserved for 'professors, teachers and students' so that they could study in peace 'uninterrupted by ordinary pleasure-seeking visitors'.

Sir Joseph and Lady Hooker, 1895. The photograph of Sir Joseph and his second wife, Hyacinth, was taken at Kew on his ninetieth birthday. It is the only known photograph of him at Kew.

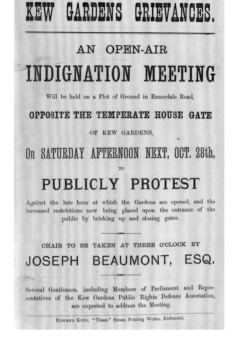

KEW GARDENS GRIEVANCES.

AN OPEN-AIR
INDIGNATION MEETING

Will be held on a Plot of Ground in Ennerdale Road,

OPPOSITE THE TEMPERATE HOUSE GATE

OF KEW GARDENS,

On SATURDAY AFTERNOON NEXT, OCT. 28th,

TO

PUBLICLY PROTEST

Against the late hour at which the Gardens are opened, and the increased restrictions now being placed upon the entrance of the public by bricking up and closing gates.

CHAIR TO BE TAKEN AT THREE O'CLOCK BY

JOSEPH BEAUMONT, ESQ.

Several Gentlemen, including Members of Parliament and Representatives of the Kew Gardens Public Rights Defence Association, are expected to address the Meeting.

EDWARD KING, "Times" Steam Printing Works, Richmond.

Kew Gardens Grievances, notice from the 'Times' Steam Printing works, Richmond c.1847. Public feelings about increased access to Kew Gardens ran so high that a Public Protest Meeting was held in 1879. This led to a debate in the House of Commons. However, Joseph Hooker managed to withstand these demands until 1883, when he conceded an extra hour a day to ordinary visitors, opening the Gardens at noon instead of 1 pm.

THE AYRTON INCIDENT

'Kew is what my father and I have made it by our sole unaided efforts; and the Ministers have for three months or more been considering a scheme for mentally altering its constitution and my position, without consulting me either directly or indirectly in the matter. I say nothing and try to think as little as possible of their utter disregard of my experience and position. I have no wish to throw up my post, but I must do so if matters go on thus.'

THE EARLIER OPENING OF KEW GARDENS — SCENE ON EASTER MONDAY OUTSIDE CUMBERLAND GATE

The Earlier Opening of Kew Gardens, cartoon, July 1877. As well as maintaining restricted opening hours, Joseph Hooker added to local public grievances by increasing the height of Kew's boundary wall. This was justified as a means of preventing workers in the Gardens from scaling the wall at all times of day to visit a local public house.

Mr. Blobbs goes down to enjoy the quiet seclusion of Gardens.

Little he knows of the Army of Tea-Touts awaiting their victims coming out.

Sad thing! He falls a victim to the Touts, and is led off in triumph to the supposed enjoyment of a shilling tea.

Tea Touts, cartoon c.1876. Another contentious issue during Joseph Hooker's tenure as director of the Royal Botanic Gardens was the lack of refreshment facilities. He even refused to let Marianne North include a small tearoom in her Gallery, saying, according to Marianne, 'it would be impossible to supply refreshments to so many (77,000 people all at once possibly on a Bank Holiday), mentioning, too, the difficulty of keeping the British Public in order'.

Portrait of Sir Joseph Hooker by E. Hook, 1909. Although he was nearly 90 by the time this picture was painted, Joseph Hooker was still active as a botanist. He was working on the genus *Impatiens* (balsams and busy lizzies), which he had first encountered in India some five decades earlier. In 1909 he published descriptions of three new species of *Impatiens*.

below **Berberis hookeri by Lilian Snelling, 1926.** This berberis was collected by Joseph Hooker in the Tambur Valley in eastern Nepal in November 1848. In *Flora Indica* published in 1855, Joseph and his co-author Thomas Thomson listed it as a variety of *Berberis wallichiana*, but the French botanist Charles Lemaire believed that it represented a distinct species and named it in his honour in 1859.

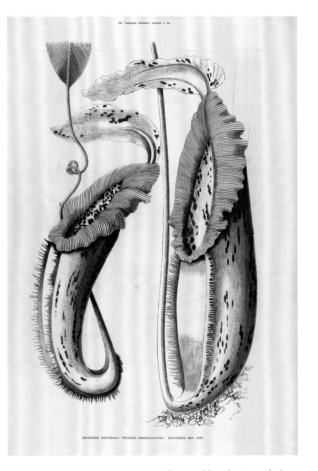

***Nepenthes northiana* by W. H. Fitch.** When the artist Marianne North showed her painting of this pitcher plant to Joseph Hooker, he realised that it was a new discovery and named the species in her honour. The Marianne North Gallery at Kew houses her painting of this plant (painting number 561) alongside over 800 others which she donated to Kew.

Onosma hookeri by Lilian Snelling, 1929. This plant was originally discovered by Joseph Hooker in the Lachen Valley in northern Sikkim in 1849. It was named in his honour by Charles Clarke, who was Superintendent of the Calcutta Botanic Gardens from 1869–71. On his retirement in 1887, Clarke continued to study Indian botany at Kew and worked with Joseph on the seven volumes of the *Flora of British India*. The plant shown here is subspecies *wardii*, named after the famous plant collector Frank Kingdon Ward, who found it in 1924 growing in the Tsangpo Valley in Eastern Tibet.

Cymbidium hookerianum by W. H. Fitch, 1866. The German botanist, Heinrich Reichenbach, one of the world's leading authorities on orchids, named this orchid after Joseph Hooker in January 1866, saying: 'an excellent name too, given with the writer's best wishes and as a gratulation for the first New Year's Day of his Kew directorship, to Dr Hooker.'

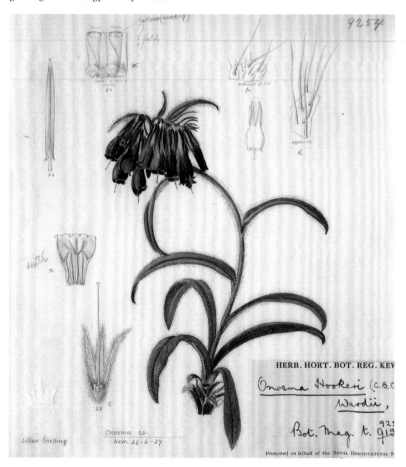

W. Fitch del et lith

Vincent Brooks Day & Son Imp

Dendrobium Hookerianum Lidl.

Rhododendron hookeri by W. H. Fitch, 1856. Dr Hooker's rhododendron, as this was commonly known, was named by Thomas Nuttall who had grown it from seed collected in Bhutan. It reflects the impact that Hooker had on rhododendron cultivation in Britain with the 25 species he introduced from Sikkim during his travels in the Himalaya.

opposite **Dendrobium hookerianum** by W. H. Fitch, 1873. Joseph Hooker found *Dendrobium hookerianum* in Sikkim in 1848 'growing on trees in hot valleys... each flower is upwards of four inches in diameter'. It was named in his honour by John Lindley, a renowned orchidologist who had been instrumental in establishing Kew as a national botanic garden, to be a 'powerful means of promoting national science'.

Impatiens lemeei, originally named as Impatiens hookeriana by W. H. Fitch, 1853. Joseph Hooker became an authority on the genus *Impatiens* after his Indian travels and this plant was named in his honour by the French botanist Augustin Léveillé. At the age of 89, Joseph wrote to Charles Darwin's son Frank: 'I have been for long years working at *Impatiens*, an enormous genus in Asia and Africa. The analysis of the dried flowers is most tedious and difficult; single flowers often taking two hours and some even a whole day to lay out for description.'

Rhodanthemum catananche by W. H. Fitch, 1874. Joseph Hooker wrote a description of *Rhodanthemum catananche* to accompany this illustration in *Curtis's Botanical Magazine*.

Welwitschia mirabilis by J .D. Hooker, 1862 in pencil and W. H. Fitch, lithograph. Joseph Hooker considered this astonishing plant 'the most wonderful, in a botanical point of view, that has been brought to light during the present century'. His father had been sent specimens collected in Angola by Frederick Welwitsch, an Austrian botanist who was exploring Portuguese colonies in West Africa. The careful diagrams of the plant and its cones, drawn by Joseph, were used as the basis of the illustrations accompanying his published description of the plant in 1864. He named the species after Welwitsch.

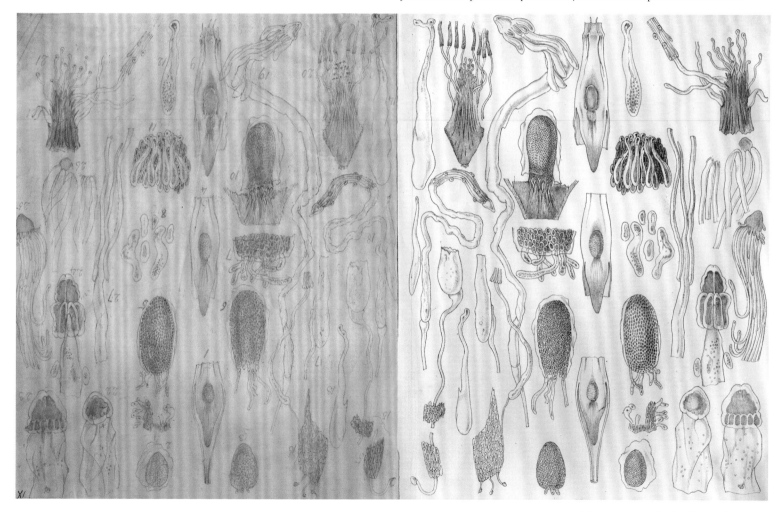

***Coffea arabica*, Company School, 19th century.** Under
Joseph Hooker's directorship, Kew played a very active role in
supporting the introduction of new crops to different parts of
the British Empire. In 1873, the Gardens initiated a scheme
to introduce disease-resistant West African coffee plants to Sri
Lanka where a fungal disease had destroyed vast areas of the
island's economically vital coffee plantations.

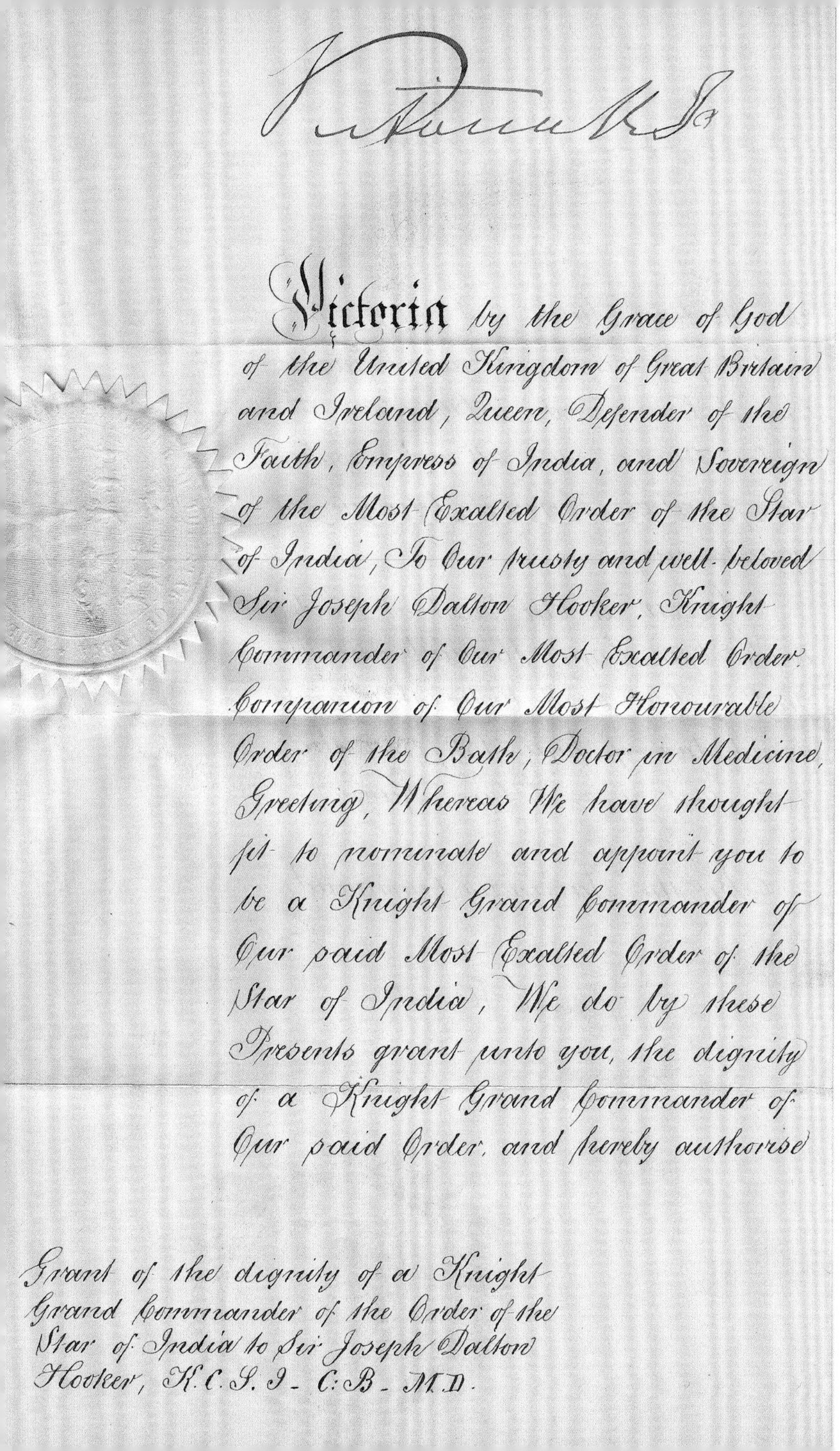

Victoria by the Grace of God of the United Kingdom of Great Britain and Ireland, Queen, Defender of the Faith, Empress of India, and Sovereign of the Most Exalted Order of the Star of India, To Our trusty and well-beloved Sir Joseph Dalton Hooker, Knight Commander of Our Most Exalted Order, Companion of Our Most Honourable Order of the Bath, Doctor in Medicine, Greeting, Whereas We have thought fit to nominate and appoint you to be a Knight Grand Commander of Our said Most Exalted Order of the Star of India, We do by these Presents grant unto you, the dignity of a Knight Grand Commander of Our said Order, and hereby authorise

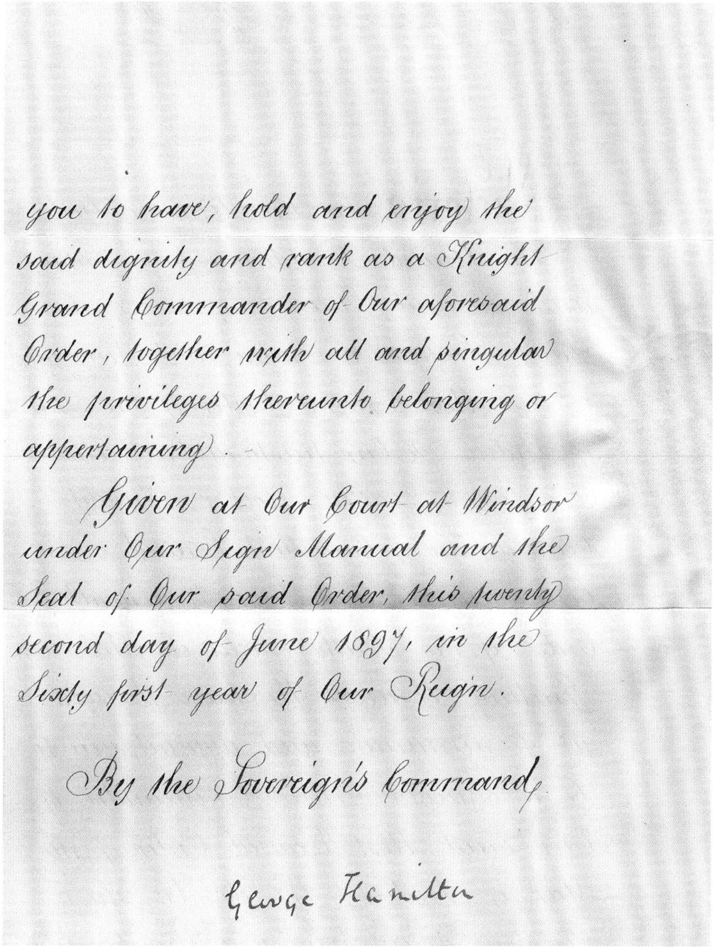

you to have, hold and enjoy the said dignity and rank as a Knight Grand Commander of Our aforesaid Order, together with all and singular the privileges thereunto belonging or appertaining.

Given at Our Court at Windsor under Our Sign Manual and the Seal of Our said Order, this twenty second day of June 1897, in the Sixty first year of Our Reign.

By the Sovereign's Command,

George Hamilton

Grant of the dignity of a Knight Grand Commander of the Order of the Star of India to Sir Joseph Dalton Hooker, K.C.S.I – C.B – M.D.

Knight Commander of the Order of the Star of India, 1877. In a letter to Charles Darwin, Sir Joseph Hooker wrote: 'I have always regarded the Star of India as the most honourable of all such distinctions... it has a flavour of hard work under difficulties, of obstacles overcome, and of brilliant deeds that is very attractive. Assuredly I would rather go down to posterity as one of the 'Star of India' than as of any other dignity whatever that the Crown can offer'. He was subsequently made Knight Grand Commander of the Star of India in Queen Victoria's Diamond Jubilee Honours in 1897.

Marble bust of Sir Joseph Hooker.

***Welwitschia mirabilis* by W. H. Fitch, 1862.**
Frederick Welwitsch described the plant he had found in letters to William Hooker: 'a dwarf tree was particularly remarkable, which with a diameter of stem often of four feet, never rose higher above the surface than one foot, and which through its entire duration, that not infrequently might exceed a century, always retained the two woody leaves which it threw up at germination.'

Scale of Inches

W. Fitch, del. et lith.

Vincent, Brooks, Imp.

FURTHER INFORMATION ABOUT JOSEPH HOOKER

Allan, M. (1967). *The Hookers of Kew*, 1785–1911. Michael Joseph, London.

Desmond, R. (1999). *Sir Joseph Dalton Hooker: Traveller and Plant Collector*. Antique Collector's Club, Woodbridge, Suffolk.

Desmond, R. (2007). *The History of the Royal Botanic Gardens, Kew. 2nd edition* Royal Botanic Gardens, Kew, London.

Endersby, J. (2008). *Imperial Nature: Joseph Hooker and the Practices of Victorian Science*. University of Chicago Press, Chicago.

Hooker, J. D. (1849-51). *The Rhododendrons of Sikkim-Himalaya*. Reeve, Benham and Reeve, London.
Available from http://www.botanicus.org/item/31753003066617

Hooker, J. D. (1855). *Himalayan Journals, or Notes of a Naturalist.*, John Murray, London.
Available from http://www.archive.org/details/himalayanjourna01hookgoog

Hooker, J. D. (1855). *Illustrations of Himalayan Plants*. L. Reeve, London.
Available from http://www.biodiversitylibrary.org/item/14650

Hooker, J. D. (1863). On *Welwitschia*, a new genus of Gnetaceae. *Transactions of the Linnean Society* 24(1): 1-64
Available from http://www.jdhooker.org.uk/PDF/welwitschia.pdf

Hooker, J. D., Ball, J. and Maw, G. (1878). *Journal of a tour in Marocco and the Great Atlas.*, Macmillan, London.
Available from http://www.biodiversitylibrary.org/item/107928#page/15/mode/1up

Huxley, L. (1918). *Life and Letters of Joseph Dalton Hooker*. John Murray, London.
Available from http://www.biodiversitylibrary.org/item/59510

Ross, J. C. (1847). *A Voyage of Discovery and Research in the Southern and Antarctic Regions During the Years 1839–43*. John Murray, London.

Williamson, M. (1984). Sir Joseph Hooker's Lecture on Insular Floras. *Biological Journal of the Linnean Society* 22: 55–77.

http://www.jdhooker.org.uk – website about J.D. Hooker, history of botany and related matters, run by Jim Endersby, science historian and senior lecturer at the University of Sussex.

Acknowledgements

This book is based on the exhibition 'Joseph Hooker: Naturalist, Traveller and More' shown in the Shirley Sherwood Gallery of Botanical Art at the Royal Botanic Gardens, Kew from November 2011–April 2012.
Many people at the Royal Botanic Gardens, Kew have contributed their expertise and assistance in shaping the exhibition and book:
Herbarium, Library, Art and Archives
Laura Giuffrida, Nicholas Hind, Christopher Mills, Mark Nesbitt, Kiri-Ross Jones, Marilyn Ward, Julia Buckley, Lyn Parker, the Directors' Correspondence Digitisation Team and other colleagues in the Art and Archives teams
Conservation, Living Collections and Estates
Colin Clubbe
Kew Publishing, Design and Photography
John Harris, Christina Harrison, Paul Little, Andrew McRobb, Michelle Payne

Kew Publishing would like to thank Jim Endersby for his assistance, especially with the timeline of Joseph Hooker's life events and travels at the front of this book.

First published in 2011 by Royal Botanic Gardens, Kew
Richmond, Surrey, TW9 3AB, UK
www.kew.org
ISBN 978 1 84246 469 4
British Library Cataloguing in Publication Data
A catalogue record for this book is available from the British Library.

Cover illustrations: main picture: Thomas Baines picture of *Welwitschia*. Inscribed in paint on verso ' The *Welwitschia mirabilis*, Nyanka Kykamkop or plant of Hykamkop or Otjitumbo Otjihooro. Stump with a head. South West Africa. T. Baines. Sketched Hykamkop May 9 1861. Painted 15 Whitehall Place, London April 10 1867.' The gentleman seen sketching the plant is Baines, his ox-wagons featured in the distance.
front flap Welwitschia mirabilis, hand coloured lithograph. Plate 5368 from *Curtis's Botanical Magazine*, 1863.
back flap Chalk portrait of Joseph Hooker by George Richmond, 1855.

Project editor: Gina Fullerlove, Publishing Design & Photography, Royal Botanic Gardens, Kew
Design, typesetting and page layout: Culver Design, based on original design by Lyn Davies

Printed in Italy by Printer Trento
For information or to purchase all Kew titles please visit www.kewbooks.com or email publishing@kew.org

Kew's mission is to inspire and deliver science-based plant conservation worldwide, enhancing the quality of life.

Kew receives half of its running costs from Government through the Department for Environment, Food and Rural Affairs (Defra). All other funding needed to support Kew's vital work comes from members, foundations, donors and commercial activities including book sales.

Joseph Hooker collected these brushes made of bamboo during his time in Tibet. He recorded their use for combing wool in his *Himalayan Journal*: 'We had much difficulty in purchasing a sufficient number of blankets (These were made of goat's wool, teazed into a satiny surface by little teazle-like brushes of bamboo.) for our people.'

Pen and ink sketch of a yak by Hooker.